Dingoes
For Kids

Amazing Animal Books
For Young Readers

By
Rachel Smith

Mendon Cottage Books
JD-Biz Corp Publishing

Read More Amazing Animal Books

Purchase at Amazon.com

Table of Contents

Introduction

The dingo is an Australian animal that has been there for a very, very long time. Lots of people hear the name, but most don't know much about them, except that they're dogs.

But what is a dingo? How is it different from pet dogs? And is it one of those crazily different Australian animals?

While the dingo is not a marsupial like the kangaroo or wallaby, it is still fairly unique, like most animals that are native to Australia. By the end of this book, you will have learned a lot more about dingoes than most people know.

What is a dingo?

A dingo is a dog, plain and simple. It's considered to be related to the gray wolf, like all dogs. Its scientific name is Canis Lupus Dingo, a sort of subspecies of wolf.

A dingo walking along.

The dingo is native to Australia, but finding a 'pure blood' dingo is nearly impossible nowadays. While many animals in Australia have been affected by animals brought by settlers and colonists, such as the effect the rabbits and rats have, dingoes were affected in a very different way.

For the dingo, the appearance of other dogs changed everything. People couldn't contain their dogs, and many of them got loose and turned wild. They joined dingo packs, and those dogs and the dingoes mated and had interbreed babies. So, most dingoes nowadays are interbreeds rather than pure dingoes.

However, it doesn't change that they are fairly unique. They have a sandy sort of color to their fur, and it's soft and bushy. Some kinds are white, and others have black and tan in their fur. Most dingoes are somewhat bi-colored, which means they have the darker reddish color and the whiter color as their fur.

They also tend to be 52 to 60 centimeters in height, and 117 to 154 from nose to tail. They also weigh about 13 to 20 kilograms. The males are typically bigger than females, but that depends on if they are the same age or not.

The dingo is mostly the dog in Australia, but it has very close relations to dogs in Southeast Asia as well. The pariah dog, for instance, is considered a dingo by most of the scientific community, as well as many of the domestic (tamed and safe around humans) dogs in that area.

Dingoes have smaller brains than wolves and other non-domesticated canines; instead, its brain is more the size of a domesticated dog's. This also shows that they are dogs more than wolves.

How do dingoes act?

Dingoes have a variety of behaviors. A lot of them are similar to dogs. This is especially true with domesticated dingoes.

A dingo pup.

Dingoes communicate with other dingoes in many ways. Sometimes, they bark, but these are very short barks compared to other dogs, and it's not very nuanced. Dingoes don't seem to prefer to bark, as they rarely do so.

Another way they communicate is howling. They do this a lot more; there are up to ten variations on their howl. The three main kinds are moans, bark-howls, and snuffs. A dingo may howl to greet other dingoes, which is a joyful expression, and to communicate among the pack.

They also growl, when feeling defensive or to show dominance. They also make a sound that is a clashing of the teeth; this is to tell pups to leave them alone, or to defend resources.

Wolves can't react to cues from humans, but dingoes can.

Dingoes mostly operate at night in warmer areas, but less so in cooler areas. They tend to do most of their hunting and other daytime sort of things during dusk and dawn.

They are also very shy around humans, for the most part. The more of a hybrid it is, though, the more it's likely to not be afraid of humans. Some dingoes move freely throughout the night in city areas; others are scared of camping grounds. So it really depends on the dingoes.

A pack with dingoes will often consist of a breeding pair and others, mostly their offspring. In really wide ranges, it may only consist of a breeding pair. The bigger the prey in the area that the dingoes are living, the bigger the pack will be.

Dingoes rely on the male leader of the pack to lead them safely. The leader will check out water sources and other such things to protect his pack. Other dingoes will usually be submissive towards him, meaning that they use posture such as flattening their ears, putting their tail down, and using a crouched position when approaching him.

Female dingoes can only be pregnant once a year. They go into a thing called heat, and that makes the male want to have a baby with them. Sometimes, they can go into heat twice a year, but they still can only get pregnant once a year.

A mama dingo can have as many as ten pups, though she typically has more like five. Mama dingoes carry their babies for about three months or a little more. Dingo females are ready to have babies at about two years old, and males can be ready anywhere from one to three years of age.

Only the Alpha pair tends to breed in a pack. These are the leaders of the pack. Alpha females will actively prevent other females from breeding, and Alpha males will put subordinate (lower ranking) males in their place. Any time a subordinate female has pups, the Alpha female will usually kill them.

Pups are typically born in the May to August time period. It would be more definite, but Australia's a big place and differs in its climate in different areas.

Sometimes, dingoes will migrate. This is only done in dire situations, and often mostly by young dingoes. If there's famine, they will go looking for food, even into human territory such as pastoral (ranch) land. They get into a lot of trouble there.

Where did dingoes come from?

There is one main theory when it comes to dingoes and their evolutionary past. Europeans who emigrated to Australia were fairly confused by the dingo, and a lot of theories were raised for it.

A dingo licking its lips.

Since dingoes are the largest placental (bears babies in the womb, with a placenta to feed them) animal in Australia, of course they would attract a lot of attention. Many people who came there didn't know what to make of it. To the Aboriginals, they were perfectly normal, but to the colonists, they looked strangely like normal dogs.

The similarities to dogs among dingoes are astonishing. Even 'pure' dingoes' DNA is so similar to dogs' that there is almost no difference.

This has led scientists to believe that, many, many years ago, dingoes were a domesticated dog. Somehow, they ended up free from their owners in Southeast Asia and ended up in Australia. It depends on when they were domesticated and when they got free, but the similarities between the dingo in Australia and the dogs in Southeast Asia are unmistakable.

This would explain why they are so close to dogs, but yet a little different and wilder. They are more closely related to modern dogs than they are to gray wolves, despite having come from them.

And, just to make it clear, there is very little difference in genetics (which is DNA, deoxyribonucleic acid) among dogs. Any given dog would be an extremely close match to a dingo, anything from a Dalmatian to a Sharpei to a Chihuahua. This is because most of the differences between dogs were made in the 1800s or so, and they simply took the dogs and bred them to pass on certain traits, until they all looked different.

At their core, dingoes are not really wolves; they are wild dogs, and are often called as such by Australians.

The dingo arrived several thousand years ago on Australia. This means it showed up long after other species had developed there. It's believed that this dog's presence led to the extinction of such native animals as the thylacine (a carnivorous marsupial), the Tasmanian devil, and the Tasmanian native hen on mainland Australia. Such creatures (with the possible exception of the thylacine) still exist on Tasmania, an island off of Australia.

However, dingoes were not as bad for native Australian fauna as the red fox would be many, many years later, and not all scientists believe they are the cause of the extinction of the thylacine, devil, and hen from mainland Australia.

The history of dingoes and humans

Dingoes, and especially the clear hybrids, are often considered a pest by the people of Australia. 'Pure' dingoes are considered a great tourist attraction, but beyond that, most dingoes are not treated all that well.

A rather white dingo.

For starters, the dingo is often in trouble with humans when it comes to livestock. Before the Europeans came, there were not that many dingoes. There was only the amount that could be supported on the prey of the land. But with the Europeans came dogs, and dogs that got free boosted the numbers of dingoes greatly.

Pretty soon, the dingo-dogs were a pest, eating livestock and messing up things. So, a lot of the history with dingoes and humans has been sad, with them often being captured or even killed because the humans don't want them in their area.

However, dingoes have been shown, when in a wild area, to be a good thing for the environment. They will hunt animals such as feral pigs and feral foxes, which are both problems for Australia, and they help to keep things in balance. They are what's called an apex hunter, meaning that they are at the top of the food chain in Australia.

To the Europeans, who did not like their sheep being attacked, the dingo seemed to be cowardly and sneaky, disappearing into the bush whenever they were caught attacking the sheep. They said it was evil, promiscuous, and had a venomous bite, so they set about to killing it at any chance they could get.

Even nowadays, this idea of the dingo being cunning and killing for fun is quoted by people in Australia as a reason for stopping them. Those who have ranches generally have little sympathy for the dingo, and have been working to get them out of their land.

There's even a dingo proof fence in the Eastern side of Australia, many kilometers wide.

Some methods used to keep the dingoes away from the paddocks:

Hanging dead dogs along the fence (not proven to work).

Using guardian animals; certain kinds of animals, such as donkeys and llamas, will fight any predator that tries to attack them (and the sheep they're with).

A reward system. This one was only used up until part of the twentieth century (the 1900s); the idea was that the government would pay for any dingo killed, because they were such a nuisance. However, this didn't really work, and the money was wasted.

Poison. A very toxic poison called strychnine is often used to kill dingoes. It is not a pleasant way to go. Because the sheep industry isn't as important as it used to be, this is used less. The way they use it is to put it in bait, and then let the dingoes find it and eat it.

Spaying and neutering. This is when it's made impossible for the animal to have babies. However, in this case, it's people's dogs that are spayed and neutered, so they don't mate with the dingoes.

These things do not always and did not always work. Dingoes are pretty clever, and there were instances of them figuring out how to do things like trigger traps and avoid poison. The main issue with poison is that it's often eaten by the wrong animal, and it's another reason that humans have stopped using them quite so much.

Dingoes are vulnerable, but not really endangered. Despite this, people continue on with their anti-dingo measures.

Culture and dingoes

Dingoes have long been an important part of Aboriginal Australian cultures. They have been used in carvings and pictures done by these people, and also in dreamtime stories. Dreamtime is a time outside of time in Aboriginal Australian mythology; it consists of stories and various figures; however, despite the supernatural nature of these figures, they are not gods. They are simply supernatural. Dreamtime is the time before there was time.

A dingo's footprint in the sand.

It seems that to the Aboriginal Australians, there was not a big difference between dogs and dingoes, and in fact, they had already adopted dogs by 1802. Dogs, and other creatures that were introduced by the colonists, were added to the Aboriginal Australian stories and ceremonies in many cases.

Another feature in Aboriginal Australian stories are the dingo-people. These are people who can turn to dingoes, or dingoes that can turn to people. Dingoes are also associated with holy places, totems, and other things. They are sometimes central characters in dreamtime stories.

However, they also show up as malicious figures in Aboriginal Australian dreamtime stories. Mamu, a specific dingo in legend, was and is said to eat children who wander too far from the campfire, being their equivalent of the boogeyman. Another is the Giant Devil Dingo, which is where all dingoes are said to come from. Its name is Gaiya, and the story with it is how it was domesticated and made to be kind to humans.

So, the presence of the dingo in the cultures of Aboriginal Australians is pretty thorough. They appear as good messengers, warning people about bad things, and as bad omens, coming to tell people bad things will happen to them and they can't stop t hem.

The dingo also features in modern, European-based Australian culture. For one thing, dingoes have been characters in TV shows, though not as prominently as their extinct rival, the thylacine.

The dingo also is used for tourism, particularly on Fraser Island, where the most 'genetically pure' dingoes live. In fact, dingoes are more protected there, and people were outraged when a pair of dingo pups was run over by a car. Dingoes are used as a symbol of the island, because they are so 'pure.' Nowhere else treats dingoes quite like the Fraser Islanders do.

Prey of dingoes

Dingoes eat various kinds of animals. They are carnivorous, which means they must survive on meat, and need a lot of protein. Their preferred way of killing prey is to bite the throat, though with bigger prey, they will usually need at least two dingoes to bring it down.

A dingo eating part of a rabbit.

One animal that dingoes eat is the kangaroo. There are a lot of them, though dingoes usually go for the juvenile (young) kangaroos. Many kangaroos die at this age for this reason. Dingo hunts of kangaroos are most successful in wide open areas, rather than in areas of dense vegetation (thick plants).

Other animals they eat include birds. Birds are tricky for a dingo to catch, given that they can't fly, but if a bird is ever too slow taking off or such, a dingo can catch it, and usually will.

They also like to steal the prey from eagles. Eagles aren't equipped to fight off dingoes, so they have to let the dingo have it once it's gone from their grasp. Dingoes don't frequently eat eagles.

Another animal that they sometimes eat is the monitor lizard. This is a big undertaking, because the monitor lizard is very large and has a poisonous bite. However, dingoes can take them down if there are three or more of them involved, and they have been observed doing so.

One problem for dingoes is one way they get food: through human trash. Some dingoes live entirely on human trash, which is a problem because this could mean they forget how to hunt properly. There's also worry that it will upset the social structures of the dingo and overall just mess them up entirely. In the United States of America, there are similar problems with animals such as bears and raccoons, and they have seen many problems with animals that live on trash there, from encounters with humans to being unable to fend for themselves in normal wilderness settings.

One more animal they often eat is the sheep. Sheep are easy targets for dingoes. Even dingoes that have never seen sheep before have been shown to be able to hunt them easily. This is because the sheep was bred not to be able to fight, but to be a food and clothing source for humans. They are not prepared to fight against any kind of predator, though a ram (male sheep with horns) may attempt to fight. This was a common problem back in medieval Europe with wolves, which are now nearly extinct in Europe. One hopes that the solution is not a similar end for the dingo.

The issue with dingoes and sheep is that sometimes, when dingoes hunt them, they get very excited by the sheep's panic and end up slaughtering them. Opponents of the dingo say this is 'killing for fun,' but that is usually not the reason that the dingo started the hunt. They are not naturally used to such easy targets, and it makes them a little giddy.

That said, they do damage a lot of sheep when they do this, which leads to their death. They don't often eat many of the sheep they hunt due to the excitement they get.

Dingoes also eat cattle, but cattle are able to fight back and often do. Sometimes, a rancher will know of an attack purely because of the scarring and marks on the steer!

In a good turn of events, though, the dingo also hunts the European rabbit, which is an invasive species. Invasive species are animals not native to the area that are rapidly taking over the place. The European rabbits definitely need to be hunted, or else they will leave nothing else for the native creatures.

Insects have even turned out to be in the dingo diet. Beetles are a part of the creatures they eat.

Lastly, in a somewhat gross fact, mother dingoes eat the urine and feces (poop and pee) of their pups so that they can keep the same amount of water inside them. This way, the female doesn't need more water in order to nurse the pups, and water is often in short supply in the dingoes' habitat.

Dingoes as pets

Dingoes are also pets in Australia. This is one step in preserving the 'pure' dingo in some parts of Australia. This keeping them as pets was illegal until fairly recently, and the dingo has been made the dog breed of Australia.

A dingo on a rock.

It is believed by some that the dingo is too wild to tame. They believe that the dingo will hurt someone if allowed to act like a normal dog. For now, it seems as though its ancient past allows it to adapt to being a pet fairly well, though there are cases where the dingoes are untameable.

The main goal with breeding and keeping the dingo is to protect its genetic purity. If humans have dingoes and keep them separate from other wild dogs, the thought is that they can save the dingo from relative extinction.

Right now, the worry is that the dingo population will be like the neanderthal population: completely absorbed by a similar species. The aim of these pet owners is to stop that from happening.

Some dingoes have been trained to help, whether in customs at airports and the like, or as sheep herders. As you can imagine, most sheep owners do not want dingoes near their sheep, but it seems they can be trained to treat sheep well.

Conclusion

The fight for the dingo is not over. It's not an entirely bad thing that they have such interbreeding; perhaps it's simply the next step in their evolution.

However, if the 'pure' dingo is to survive, then it will take a big effort from the Australian people. Hopefully, we will see them rise to the occasion in the future.

Author Bio

Rachel Smith is a young author who enjoys animals. Once, she had a rabbit who was very nervous, and chewed through her leash and tried to escape. She's also had several pet mice, who were the funniest little animals to watch. She lives in Ohio with her family and writes in her spare time.

Publisher

JD-Biz Corp

P O Box 374

Mendon, Utah 84325

http://www.jd-biz.com/

Mendon Cottage Books
P O Box 374, Mendon Utah 84325

Top Ten Dog Breeds For Kids

Amazing Animal Books For Young Readers

Kisha Bennett & John Davidson

German Shepherds

Dog Books for Kids

K. Bennett

Bulldogs

Dog Books for Kids

K. Bennett

Dachshund

Dog Books for Kids

K. Bennett

Poodles

Labrador Retrievers

Rottweilers

Boxers

Dog Books for Kids

K. Bennett

Dog Books for Kids

K. Bennett

Dog Books for Kids

K. Bennett

Dog Books for Kids

K. Bennett

Golden Retrievers

Dog Books for Kids

K. Bennett

Puppies

Dog Books For Kids

Amazing Animal Books

By John Davidson

Beagles

Dog Books for Kids

K. Bennett

Yorkshire Terriers

Dog Books for Kids

K. Bennett

Dogs
Top Ten Dog Breeds For Kids

Amazing Animal Books For Young Readers

Zahra Jazeel & John Davidson

Cats
For Kids

Amazing Animal Books For Young Readers

K. Bennett & John Davidson

Foxes
For Kids

Amazing Animal Books For Young Readers

Zahra Jazeel & John Davidson

Wolves
For Kids

Amazing Animal Books For Young Readers

By John Davidson and Virginia Fidler

Made in the USA
San Bernardino, CA
17 April 2016